# Celebrations in My World

# Hanukkah

**Crabtree Publishing Company**

www.crabtreebooks.com

# Crabtree Publishing Company

## www.crabtreebooks.com

Coordinating editor: Chester Fisher
Series editor: Susan Labella
Author: Molly Aloian
Project manager: Kavita Lad (Q2AMEDIA)
Art direction: Dibakar Acharjee (Q2AMEDIA)
Cover design: Ranjan Singh (Q2AMEDIA)
Design: Ruchi Sharma (Q2AMEDIA)
Photo research: Sejal Sehgal Wani (Q2AMEDIA)
Editor: Kelley MacAulay
Copy editor: Adrianna Morganelli
Proofreader: Crystal Sikkens
Project editor: Robert Walker
Production coordinator: Katherine Kantor
Font management: Mike Golka
Prepress technicians: Katherine Kantor, Ken Wright

Photographs:
Cover: Jani Bryson/Istockphoto; Title page: Brand
X Pictures/Jupiter Images; P4: Boris Katsman/
Shutterstock; P5: Joe Griffin/Image Works;
P6: Martine Oger/Shutterstock; P7: Mary Evans
Picture Library/Alamy; P9: Joel Carillet/Istockphoto;
P10: Clifford Shirley/Istockphoto; P11: Israelimages/
Rex Features; P13: Comstock Images/Jupiter Images;
P15: Steven Allan/Istockphoto; P17: Sean Locke/
Istockphoto; P19: Matthias Wassermann/Istockphoto;
P20: Israel Images/Alamy; P23: Jeff Greenberg/
The Image Works; P24: Scott/Bigstockphoto;
P25: Scott Rothstein/Shutterstock; P26: Jani
Bryson/Istockphoto; P29: Associated Press;
P31: Corbis/Jupiter Images

Library and Archives Canada Cataloguing in Publication

Aloian, Molly
    Hanukkah / Molly Aloian.

(Celebrations in my world)
Includes index.
ISBN 978-0-7787-4283-8 (bound).--ISBN 978-0-7787-4301-9 (pbk.)

    1. Hanukkah--Juvenile literature. I. Title. II. Series.

BM695.H3A46 2008        j296.4'35        C2008-903115-6

Library of Congress Cataloging-in-Publication Data

Aloian, Molly.
    Hanukkah / Molly Aloian.
        p. cm. -- (Celebrations in my world)
    Includes index.
    ISBN-13: 978-0-7787-4301-9 (pbk. : alk. paper)
    ISBN-10: 0-7787-4301-2 (pbk. : alk. paper)
    ISBN-13: 978-0-7787-4283-8 (reinforced library binding : alk. paper)
    ISBN-10: 0-7787-4283-0 (reinforced library binding : alk. paper)
    1. Hanukkah--Juvenile literature. I. Title. II. Series.

BM695.H3A6593 2009
296.4'35--dc22
                                          2008021205

## Crabtree Publishing Company

www.crabtreebooks.com        1-800-387-7650

**Published in Canada**
**Crabtree Publishing**
616 Welland Ave.
St. Catharines, ON
L2M 5V6

**Published in the United States**
**Crabtree Publishing**
PMB16A
350 Fifth Ave., Suite 3308
New York, NY 10118

**Published in the United Kingdom**
**Crabtree Publishing**
White Cross Mills
High Town, Lancaster
LA1 4XS

**Published in Australia**
**Crabtree Publishing**
386 Mt. Alexander Rd.
Ascot Vale (Melbourne)
VIC 3032

# Contents

# What is Hanukkah?

Hanukkah is a holiday celebrated by people of the Jewish religion. The Jewish religion is called Judaism. Jewish people celebrate Hanukkah each year in late November or early December. The exact dates change from year to year. Hanukkah lasts eight days and eight nights. It begins at sunset on the first day.

Many Jewish people read religious words from scrolls.

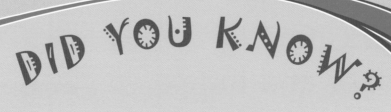

*DID YOU KNOW?*

*Millions of Jewish people live in countries all over the world.*

During Hanukkah, Jewish people living today remember their **ancestors** who lived long ago. Jewish people today also remember how Hanukkah became such a special holiday.

Many Jewish parents teach their children about Hanukkah.

5

# A Miracle!

Hanukkah celebrates the story of the Maccabees. Over 2,000 years ago, an evil Greek king named Antiochus would not allow Jewish people to practice their religion. He wanted the Jews to adopt Greek ways. He took over their **temple** in Jerusalem, Israel. A small group of brave Jewish soldiers fought back against the king's huge army.

This map shows Israel in the Middle east.

*DID YOU KNOW?*

*Judah Maccabee is known as one of the greatest warriors in Jewish history. His bravery has inspired many writers, artists, and composers.*

A man named Judah Maccabee was the leader of the Jewish soldiers. His soldiers were called the Maccabees. After many long battles, the Maccabees won back their temple. They believed their victory was a **miracle**. Jewish people were free to practice their religion once again!

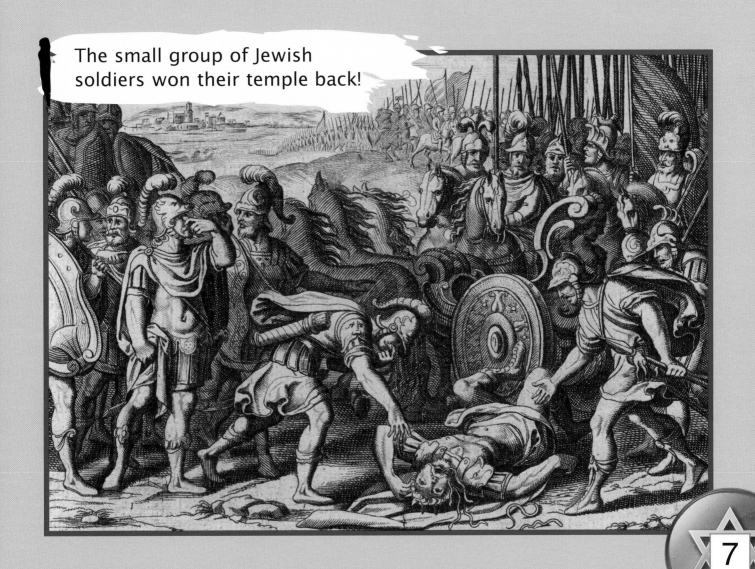

The small group of Jewish soldiers won their temple back!

# Rededication

Following this victory, the Jewish people cleaned out their temple. They swept and scrubbed until the temple was clean. They prayed, sang, and celebrated for eight nights and eight days. The word Hanukkah means "rededication" in the **Hebrew** language. The word "dedication" means to set something apart for a special purpose or reason. So, "rededication" means to once again set something apart for a special purpose or reason.

## DID YOU KNOW?

*The Maccabees fought a huge army for three years before they were able to take back their temple.*

The Maccabees fought in Jerusalem to keep their traditions and beliefs.

# Sacred Oil

During Hanukkah, people also remember a story from the first Hanukkah celebration. This story is about a miracle that occurred with the Jews' **sacred** oil. In the story, the Jews wanted to light a special oil lamp using the sacred oil. They did not have enough oil to burn for all eight days and eight nights of the celebration.

● The tiny bit of oil lasted for eight nights.

## DID YOU KNOW?

*The soldiers poured oil into a lamp and it burned for eight days. They celebrated for as long as the oil burned. This is why today the Hanukkah celebration last for eight nights.*

The Jews needed more oil. They started to burn what they had. Then a miracle occurred! The tiny bit of oil burned for eight nights!

A Hanukkah lamp burns to **commemorate** the miracle of the oil.

# Family and Friends

During Hanukkah, Jewish families and friends gather together. Some families invite people who live alone to join them in their Hanukkah celebrations. During these celebrations, people light candles, eat special foods, and sing songs. People also express their feelings to their families and friends. They tell their loved ones that they are important and cared for. Many people express these feelings by sending cards.

### DID YOU KNOW?

*Many Jewish people believe that they must try to be good people at all times. They encourage their families and friends to think of others.*

Celebrating Hanukkah reminds Jewish people of one of the most important times in their history.

13

# The Menorah

On each night of Hanukkah, people light candles. The candles are held in a candle holder called a **menorah**. The menorah is a symbol of the Jewish faith. A symbol stands for or represents something else. The menorah is a symbol for the state of Israel. The menorah holds nine candles. There is one candle for each of the eight nights. The ninth candle is called a *shamash*. People light the *shamash* first then use it to light the other eight candles.

DID YOU KNOW?

*Menorahs come in many sizes. Some menorahs are over ten feet (three meters) high and over ten feet (three meters) wide!*

The *shamash* is usually higher or lower than the other candles in the menorah.

# Lighting Candles

On the first night of Hanukkah, an adult lights the *shamash* with a match. Then, a child uses the *shamash* to light one other candle. On the second night, a child lights two candles with the *shamash*. On the third night, three candles are lit, and so on. On the eighth night, all nine candles are lit. People burn candles to provide light on dark, cold winter nights during Hanukkah. They also light candles to help them remember the eight nights when people celebrated in the temple.

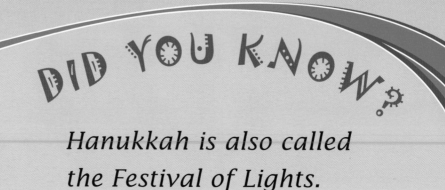

## DID YOU KNOW?

*Hanukkah is also called the Festival of Lights.*

Some people display their Hanukkah menorahs outside their homes or in windows. Menorahs are sometimes even displayed in parks within towns and cities.

The word *shamash* means servant or helper in Hebrew.

17

# Saying Prayers

Some people say prayers when they light the candles on each night of Hanukkah. They may pray out loud or quietly to themselves. They pray because they are grateful to be able to celebrate Hanukkah and the Jewish faith. One prayer people say during Hanukkah is called "Hanerot Halalu." People say this prayer after lighting the candles in the menorah. Some Jewish people wear shawls while they pray. The prayer shawl is called a *tallis*.

DID YOU KNOW?

*Jewish people read a **holy** book called the Torah. The Torah includes five books of Jewish law and learning. The word Torah means "teachings" in the Hebrew language.*

Jewish people pray to **honor** the miracles that happened long ago.

# Giving Blessings

Most people say the blessings before they light the candles. Other people say the blessings after the candles are lit.

Some people also say **blessings** during Hanukkah. Blessings are short prayers said to offer thanks or happiness to others. To say blessings, family members gather around the menorah at sundown. They usually say the blessings before lighting the menorah. People say two blessings on each night of Hanukkah. The first blessing is said to God, to thank Him for telling them to light the Hanukkah lights. The second is said to God to thank Him for making past miracles happen. Blessings of joy are said when the menorah is first lit.

## DID YOU KNOW?

*Each night, the menorah should remain lit for at least 30 minutes.*

# Eating Foods

During Hanukkah, people eat foods made with oil to celebrate the miracle of the oil. They make potato pancakes called *latkes* and fry them in oil. The potato pancakes are made with potatoes, onions, flour, and eggs. People also eat donuts filled with jelly called *sufganiyot*. The donuts are also fried in oil. People often make these foods with their families and friends and enjoy the meals together.

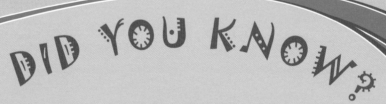

DID YOU KNOW?

*Jewish people have to be **kosher**, which means "acceptable" or "clean." To remain kosher, some Jewish people follow special rules about what they eat and how the foods are prepared.*

People celebrate Hanukkah by preparing and eating food together. They often dip *latkes* in applesauce or sour cream.

23

# Spinning Dreidels

During Hanukkah, some children like to play with **dreidels**. A dreidel is a spinning top with four sides. On each side of the dreidel, there is a different Hebrew letter. There are different kinds of dreidels. Some dreidels are wooden, whereas others are plastic. Children play fun games using dreidels. Turn the page to learn how to play the game!

● Children play a game with dreidels.

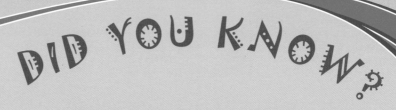

DID YOU KNOW?

*The letters on a dreidel are part of a Hebrew phrase that means "A Great Miracle Happened There".*

24

Many popular Hanukkah songs mention dreidels, including the song called "I Have a Little Dreidel." This song is about making your own dreidel and playing with it.

Each letter on a dreidel means something different in the dreidel game.

# The Dreidel Game

It is the boy's turn
to spin the dreidel.

Children love to play the dreidel game. Four to six players put one item, such as a piece of candy, into a pile called the pot. Players then take turns spinning the dreidel. After spinning the dreidel, the player looks at the Hebrew letter that lands face up to find out what to do next. If the *gimel* is face up, the player takes all of the candies. If the *hey* is face up, the player takes half of the candies. If the *nun* is face up, the player takes nothing. Finally, if the *shin* lands face up, the player must put two more candies into the pot. When someone wins the whole pot, the game is over.

## DID YOU KNOW?

*People play dreidel games with nuts, raisins, beans, or pieces of candy.*

# Singing Songs

Families and friends sing songs during Hanukkah. Some people sing a **hymn** called "Ma'oz Tzur." A hymn is a kind of song. "Ma'oz Tzur" is written in Hebrew. People sing songs as they light the menorah or just after they light the menorah. The words in the songs help remind people of the events they are celebrating. Some people sing the Hanukkah blessings over the candles instead of reciting them. They can sing any way they wish!

## DID YOU KNOW?

*Some children also put on Hanukkah plays. They wear costumes and perform the plays for their friends and families.*

Hanukkah songs can be sung alone or in groups.

# Giving Gifts

Many children give and receive presents during Hanukkah. Some children receive a present on each night of Hanukkah. Others receive one big present on the last night of the holiday. Children may also receive money. People do not only receive gifts, though. Hanukkah is a time to think of others who are in need. People give **charity** to those who are in need. Charity can be money, clothing, or other helpful items. The Jewish word for charity is *tzedakah*.

## DID YOU KNOW?

*Some children receive chocolates that are shaped and stamped like coins and wrapped in gold or silver foil. They use the chocolate coins to play the dreidel game.*

This child is receiving
gifts for Hanukkah.

# Glossary

**ancestors** The people from whom an individual or group is descended

**blessing** Asking for care and protection for something

**charity** Giving help to the poor and to those who are suffering

**commemorate** To remember and celebrate

**dreidel** A small, four-sided spinning top

**Hebrew** Language of Jewish people

**holy** For the worship of God

**honor** To treat with respect

**kosher** Food prepared according to Jewish ceremonial law

**menorah** A candlestick used in Jewish ceremonies

**miracle** An extraordinary or unusual event

**hymn** A religious song or poem

**sacred** Describing something that is very special

**temple** A building in ancient Jerusalem that was the main place for Jewish people to pray and worship

# Index

32

Printed in the U.S.A.